Nate Maerz

Celebration Place™
Journal
52 WEEK

Group

LOVELAND, CO

group.com

Group resources really work!

This Group resource incorporates our R.E.A.L. approach to ministry. It reinforces a growing friendship with Jesus, encourages long-term learning, and results in life transformation, because it's

Relational
Learner-to-learner interaction enhances learning and builds Christian friendships.

Experiential
What learners experience through discussion and action sticks with them up to 9 times longer than what they simply hear or read.

Applicable
The aim of Christian education is to equip learners to be both hearers and doers of God's Word.

Learner-based
Learners understand and retain more when the learning process takes into consideration how they learn best.

CELEBRATION PLACE™ JOURNAL
A CELEBRATE RECOVERY® RESOURCE

Copyright © 2014 Group Publishing, Inc

Visit our website: **group.com**

ISBN 978-1-4707-1328-7
10 9 8 7 6 5 4 3 2   22 21 20 19 18 17 16 15 14
Printed in U.S.A.

WELCOME TO

Celebration
Place.

We're excited that you're joining us on this special journey. While the people you came with are at Celebrate Recovery®, we'll meet here to make new friends, share ideas, play games, sing songs, create crafts, watch videos and movies—and each week we'll learn about the same things the adults learn about during their meeting time. And most important of all, we'll learn about God's amazing love for us.

You'll use your Celebration Place™ Journal each week to record your thoughts and feelings. And at the end of each meeting, you can tear out your journal page and take home the page to help you and your parents talk about what you've learned.

We look forward to being with you—learning, growing, and doing lots of fun things together!

Note to the Leader: Distribute the Celebration Place Journals before small groups each week, so kids can use them to reflect on their experiences. At the end of the meeting, have kids each tear out that week's Celebration Place Journal page to take home as a conversation-starter for families.

Celebration Place Journal

Sad   Mad   Glad   Afraid

This week was...

_____

_____

Write About It...

1. _____

_____

2. _____

_____

3. _____

_____

Pray About It...

_____

_____

_____

WEEK 1: WELCOME TO CELEBRATION PLACE

THIS WEEK AT CELEBRATION PLACE

Our leaders answered fun questions like, "If you were paid a million dollars, would you take a bath in a tub full of leeches?" Kids then shared something about themselves and their hopes for their families as a result of Celebrate Recovery. They made new friends, learned one another's names, and discovered things they have in common through fun games. They also learned the child version of the Serenity Prayer, which we'll close with each week.

Parents: Share with your child one thing you hope will happen for your family because of Celebrate Recovery. If you saw God already at work in the thing you're hoping for today, describe to your child the encouragement you feel. Invite your child to share something he or she is hoping will happen because of Celebration Station, too.

 God, thank you for leading us to Celebration Place and Celebrate Recovery. Thank you that you're with us on our journey. In Jesus' name. Amen.

Celebration Place Journal

Sad   Mad   Glad   Afraid

This week was...

_____

_____

✏ Write About It...

1. _____

_____

2. _____

_____

3. _____

_____

🙏 Pray About It...

_____

_____

_____

WEEK 2: DENIAL

Key Verse: "Happy are those who know they are spiritually poor"
(Matthew 5:3).

THIS WEEK AT CELEBRATION PLACE

Your child learned that denial is when we're not being honest on the outside about what's really going on in the inside. It's a lot like wearing a mask. Children also learned that denying what's true can make us feel trapped in our problems and stuck in our guilt. We have to face our problems so we can get out of the trap. We all have problems and God can help us with our problems, but we have to admit we have a problem first.

Parents: Talk about a mask you remember wearing as a child. Perhaps it was a Halloween mask such as a superhero or a princess. Tell your child about the mask and why you chose that mask. Then talk to your child about how it feels for you now that God is helping you take off masks in real life so you can be honest. Let your child know that you're a safe person for him or her to take off a mask and talk about feelings. Then follow through by listening without judgment.

 God, help us be honest on the outside with how we feel on the inside. Thank you for healing us. In Jesus' name. Amen.

Celebration Place Journal

Sad   Mad   Glad   Afraid

This week was...

_____

_____

✏ Write About It...

1. _____

_____

2. _____

_____

3. _____

_____

🙏 Pray About It...

_____

_____

_____

WEEK 3: DENIAL

**Key Verse: "Happy are those who know they are spiritually poor"
(Matthew 5:3).**

THIS WEEK AT CELEBRATION PLACE

Your child learned that holding onto hurts is painful and takes a
lot of energy. Children also learned that hanging onto pain causes
them to live in denial, which leads to more hurts, hang-ups, and
habits. Letting go takes work and requires us to be honest about
our hurts. Even if we can't change the things that cause our pain,
being honest about our feelings helps us stay healthy. Children discovered that once they get past denial and acknowledge pain, they
can pray and ask God to help them let go of the hurt.

**Parents: Talk about a time you struggled to let go of
something painful.** Maybe you had a hard time letting go of sad-
ness after losing a pet or moving away from your friends or relatives.
Let your child know that sometimes, even as adults, we hold onto not
only good things but also bad things, including painful memories,
because we don't know how to let go. Explain that God will always
listen and that God sent you, too, to listen and help your child let go
of hurts. Then leave the door open for discussion.

 *God, thank you for loving us and for sending others to help
us let go of painful memories. Help us face things that cause
us pain, even if we can't change them. In Jesus' name. Amen.*

Celebration Place Journal

Sad **Mad** **Glad** **Afraid**

This week was...

_____
_____

✏ Write About It...

1. _____
_____
2. _____
_____
3. _____
_____

🙏 Pray About It...

_____
_____
_____

WEEK 4: POWERLESS

**Key Verse: "Happy are those who know they are spiritually poor"
(Matthew 5:3).**

THIS WEEK AT CELEBRATION PLACE

Your child learned that Jesus calms our fears in the storms of life
and that we're powerless without him. Children experienced the
story of how Jesus taught this lesson to his disciples who called out
to him for help when a storm threatened to capsize their boat. By
putting their trust in Jesus, the disciples were able to feel his awesome power. Children discovered that they're powerless to calm
their inner "storms" without God and they can call on God when
they're afraid.

**Parents: Tell your child about a time you were caught
in a thunderstorm or blizzard.** Recall the details of the
storm and your fears at the time to your child. Then talk about
how it feels to know you don't have to face the storms in your life
alone—that God is always there to listen and provide help, sometimes through other people such as the friends you're making at
Celebrate Recovery and Celebration Place. Affirm your willingness
to listen to your child's fears about the storms in his or her life, and
then listen without dismissing your child's very real concerns.

*God, thank you for being with us, helping us with our fears,
and providing others to support us. We're powerless without
you. In Jesus' name. Amen.*

Celebration Place Journal

Sad　　**Mad**　　**Glad**　　**Afraid**

This week was...

_____
_____

✏️ write About It...

1. _____
_____
2. _____
_____
3. _____
_____

🙏 Pray About It...

_____
_____
_____

WEEK 5: POWERLESS

Key Verse: "Happy are those who know they are spiritually poor" (Matthew 5:3).

THIS WEEK AT CELEBRATION PLACE

Your child learned that while we often try to solve problems on our own, we're powerless to do this without God. Sometimes people even try to escape their pain by turning to "solutions" that really hurt more than they help—such as overeating, smoking, or drinking. Trying to solve problems on our own causes us to live in the dark. Children learned that admitting we need God to control our lives is like turning on the light. Part of giving control to God means trusting his timing, which isn't always "right away."

Parents: Talk about how you felt to actually be in the dark as a child. Ask your child what it's like to be in the dark. Then talk to your child about how you're asking God into your life to take control of problems you thought you could fix on your own. Discuss with your child a way that God's light could shine on his or her life.

 God, we're powerless without you and we ask you to shine your light in our lives. Thank you for giving us strength. In Jesus' name. Amen.

Celebration Place Journal

Sad   Mad   Glad   Afraid

This week was...

_____

_____

Write About It...

1. _____

_____

2. _____

_____

3. _____

_____

Pray About It...

_____

_____

_____

WEEK 6: HOPE

Key Verse: "Happy are those who mourn, for they shall be comforted" (Matthew 5:4).

THIS WEEK AT CELEBRATION PLACE

Your child learned that only Jesus can give hope for something better, even though some people might turn to food, drugs, or alcohol as they try to deal with their hurts. Children discussed how God is the ultimate source of all things, even things that appear to be man-made. When we understand the depth of God's power, we realize we can put our hope in him whenever we need help dealing with hurts and making changes.

Parents: Share about a change you had to make, such as learning a new computer program or choosing foods to fit a new, healthy lifestyle. Describe the challenges and how strange it felt to make the change. Then talk about how it can be scary to hope for the best when we make a change in life—how we might think it would be easier to just go back to the old way of doing things. Explain how you're hoping for something better in your life right now and putting your hope in God, who has the power to help us grow. Let your child know that he or she can share concerns about changes with you.

 God, please help us put our hope in you and have faith that you will be with us through changes in life. Thank you for always being with us. In Jesus' name. Amen.

Celebration Place Journal

Sad   Mad   Glad   Afraid

This week was...

_____

_____

✏️ Write About It...

1. _____

_____

2. _____

_____

3. _____

_____

🙏 Pray About It...

_____

_____

_____

WEEK 7: HOPE

Key Verse: "Happy are those who mourn, for they shall be comforted" (Matthew 5:4).

THIS WEEK AT CELEBRATION PLACE

Your child learned a lesson about putting hope in God's power: Even a small amount of faith—as small as a mustard seed—is enough for God to move the mountains in your child's life. When change is slow, children might begin to doubt whether they can put their hope in God. But they discovered that God provides evidence of his existence everywhere, from nature to newborn babies.

Parents: Share about a time you doubted a path you were following. Maybe you were on a hike or driving around an unfamiliar town with directions that weren't clear to you. How did you find your way? Then talk to your child about how you're putting your faith in God to help you find your way in life. Describe some of the signs you've noticed of God working in your life and how those signs are giving you hope. Ask your child what signs of God he or she has noticed lately.

God, thank you for renewing our hope by sending us signs that you're here on Earth with us. Help us follow you every day. In Jesus' name. Amen.

Celebration Place Journal

Sad   Mad   Glad   Afraid

This week was...

_____
_____

✏️ Write About It...

1. _____
_____
2. _____
_____
3. _____
_____

🙏 Pray About It...

_____
_____
_____

WEEK 8: SPECIAL EVENT

Key Verse: "He leads the humble in doing right, teaching them his way" (Psalm 25:9).

THIS WEEK AT CELEBRATION PLACE

Your child learned about the importance of being humble by watching and discussing the movie *The Emperor's New Groove*. Jesus wants us to put the needs of others first and be willing to serve. We can't do that if we're rude or full of pride. The emperor finally learned that it's our inside that counts, but not until he was humbled by being turned into a llama! After the movie, children practiced serving others.

Parents: Tell your child about a time someone served you when you really needed help. Maybe someone made you dinner when you were sick or helped you fix your car. Describe how valuable the person's service was to you. Explain that being humble also means asking for help when we need it and that God sends others to help us. Ask your child about his or her favorite way to serve others.

God, help us remember that everything we have is a gift from you, even our special talents. Please help us to stay humble. In Jesus' name. Amen.

Celebration Place Journal

Sad   **Mad**   **Glad**   **Afraid**

This week was...

_____

_____

✏️ Write About It...

1. _____

_____

2. _____

_____

3. _____

_____

🙏 Pray About It...

_____

_____

_____

WEEK 9: PEACE (SANITY)

Key Verse: "Happy are those who mourn, for they shall be comforted" (Matthew 5:4).

THIS WEEK AT CELEBRATION PLACE

Your child learned that even when life feels chaotic, Jesus is here to bring peace. Children played a game where they had to dodge paper wads from all directions, and they experienced how challenges are easier with help. They recognized positive traits about themselves and learned that God sees them and loves them just the way they are.

Parents: Tell your child about a place that's peaceful for you. You might relax in your garden, for example. If you feel God's presence in your peaceful place, describe that as well. Let your child share about his or her peaceful place, too. Then talk to your child about how you let God help you when chaos surrounds you. Reassure your child that he or she isn't responsible for the chaos that may sometimes exist in your home life.

 God, help us seek you when we need peace from the chaos. Thank you for being in all places so we can always find you. In Jesus' name. Amen.

Celebration Place Journal

Sad   Mad   Glad   Afraid

This week was...

_____
_____

write About It...

1. _____
_____
2. _____
_____
3. _____
_____

Pray About It...

_____
_____
_____

WEEK 10: PEACE (SANITY)

Key Verse: "Happy are those who mourn, for they shall be comforted" (Matthew 5:4).

THIS WEEK AT CELEBRATION PLACE

Your child learned that we can't feel better all by ourselves when life is overwhelming or gives us "crushing" disappointments. We're powerless to change without believing in God and receiving his peace. Trusting others can bring us peace at times; trusting God never fails. Children learned about the transformation that happens when we follow Jesus—similar to how a caterpillar becomes a butterfly.

Parents: Describe a time you felt overwhelmed. Maybe you had a school or work deadline looming, or you were planning a party and really needed help. Then explain how you're learning to trust God for peace when situations feel overwhelming and even crushing. Let your child know you understand childhood pressures can be overwhelming, too, and then listen if he or she wants to share.

 God, help us turn to you for peace when we feel overwhelmed. Thank you for giving us new life in you, just like a peaceful butterfly. In Jesus' name. Amen.

Celebration Place Journal

Sad　　**Mad**　　**Glad**　　**Afraid**

This week was...

_____
_____

✏️ Write About It...

1. _____
_____
2. _____
_____
3. _____
_____

🙏 Pray About It...

_____
_____
_____

WEEK 11: TURNAROUND (TURN)

Key Verse: "Happy are the meek" (Matthew 5:5).

THIS WEEK AT CELEBRATION PLACE

Your child learned about trusting God. The more children get to know God, the more they'll see that everything God says in the Bible is true. Children also discovered what it means to repent: to turn and go the other way. Our lives get messy with sin when we let it take over and when we make wrong choices rather than turning to God with our problems. Children learned about accepting Jesus' gift of forgiveness when they sin.

Parents: Talk about a time you turned around and went the other way—and the outcome. Perhaps you were driving and made a U-turn. Or perhaps you changed your mind about something. Encourage your child to share about a changed decision in his or her life—and the outcome. Commit to one another to turn around and go the other way this week if tempted to sin.

God, thank you for being so trustworthy, even when we can't see you with our eyes. Help us remember to turn to you when life gets messy. In Jesus' name. Amen.

Celebration Place Journal

Sad **Mad** **Glad** **Afraid**

This week was...

_____

_____

✏️ write About It...

1. _____

_____

2. _____

_____

3. _____

_____

🙏 Pray About It...

_____

_____

_____

WEEK 12: TURNAROUND (TURN)

Key Verse: "Happy are the meek" (Matthew 5:5).

THIS WEEK AT CELEBRATION PLACE

Children learned that they don't have to walk around carrying heavy burdens and stumbling under the load of sinful behavior. We all sin, but Jesus is willing to carry the pains and burdens for us. Children heard the prodigal son's story, whose father loved and forgave him when he returned home after making many bad choices—the same way our heavenly Father loves and forgives us.

Parents: Describe a time you had to ask for forgiveness. Maybe you were ungrateful like the prodigal son or disobedient to a teacher. How did it feel to carry that burden? to let go of it? Did the person forgive you when you apologized? Then explain how it feels to know you make good choices and let God take over the weight and burden of bad choices you've made in the past. Let your child know that your love is unconditional and that you're willing to listen if he or she has burdens to unload.

 God, thank you for your gift of forgiveness through your Son, Jesus. Help us to come to you when we make bad choices. In Jesus' name. Amen.

Celebration Place Journal

Sad   Mad   Glad   Afraid

This week was...

_____

_____

✏️ Write About It...

1. _____

_____

2. _____

_____

3. _____

_____

🙏 Pray About It...

_____

_____

_____

WEEK 13: ACTION

Key Verse: "Happy are the meek" (Matthew 5:5).

THIS WEEK AT CELEBRATION PLACE

Your child learned about choosing between right and wrong. Sometimes it's easier to follow peer pressure and the ways of the world. But God wants us to take action and choose to let him take control and mold us in his image. Children talked about the importance of living and taking action in the present rather than worrying about the past or the future.

Parents: Talk about a time you had to choose whether or not to follow a crowd. Maybe your friends were sneaking into an R-rated movie or someone was giving out answers to a test. Describe how you felt after you did or didn't resist the peer pressure. Ask your child when he or she finds it especially difficult to choose what's right. Then talk with your child about how you can both take action to live in the present and give every day to God.

 God, we know you have awesome plans for us! Help us take action in choosing your way...every day. Thank you for helping us change. In Jesus' name. Amen.

Celebration Place Journal

Sad **Mad** **Glad** **Afraid**

This week was...

_____
_____

Write About It...

1. _____
_____
2. _____
_____
3. _____
_____

Pray About It...

_____
_____
_____

WEEK 14: PRAYER STATIONS

Key Verse: "Happy are the meek" (Matthew 5:5).

THIS WEEK AT CELEBRATION PLACE

Your child learned that Jesus will take whatever faith he or she has to give—even if it seems like just a tiny amount—and make it grow. The example children heard was the story of how Jesus took the five loaves of bread and two fish that the disciples had to share and fed 5,000 people with it. Children spent time quietly talking with God at three prayer stations: reflecting on Jesus' suffering, praying for someone who needs special prayer today, and experiencing God's cool refreshment and cleansing.

Parents: Talk about a time you only had a little to give.

Perhaps you only had a little money to spend on Christmas gifts, or you could only spare an hour to visit an elderly relative. Tell your child how this little amount was multiplied into something unexpected or memorable. Then explain how it feels to know that what you have to give God is enough and how God is making your faith grow. Help your child think of a time Jesus changed a little bit of hope into something wonderful for your family.

 God, we can't see you but we can see the good works you're doing in our lives. Thank you for hearing even the smallest of our prayers. In Jesus' name. Amen.

Celebration Place Journal

Sad   Mad   Glad   Afraid

This week was...

_____

_____

Write About It...

1. _____

_____

2. _____

_____

3. _____

_____

Pray About It...

_____

_____

_____

WEEK 15: HONESTY (MORAL)

Key Verse: "Happy are the pure in heart" (Matthew 5:8).

THIS WEEK AT CELEBRATION PLACE

Your child learned about being honest and having a pure heart. Children acted out scenes from the parable of the sower in Matthew 13:1-9 and learned that whatever we plant in our lives will grow. If we plant hurts and hang-ups, we'll grow habits. Children also talked about the importance of looking forward rather than getting stuck in the past.

Parents: Tell your child about something you've planted. Describe whether it grew well or not—and why. Then tell your child some wonderful things you've seen growing in his or her life recently. Encourage your child to keep watering those things with God's love and letting God's truth shine on them.

 God, please help us keep growing the wonderful things in our lives with the help of your love. Thank you for hearing our prayers and planting great things in us. In Jesus' name. Amen.

Celebration Place Journal

Sad   Mad   Glad   Afraid

This week was...

_____

_____

✏️ Write About It...

1. _____

_____

2. _____

_____

3. _____

_____

🙏 Pray About It...

_____

_____

_____

WEEK 16: HONESTY (MORAL)

Key Verse: "Happy are the pure in heart" (Matthew 5:8).

THIS WEEK AT CELEBRATION PLACE

Your child learned about why honesty is key to having a pure heart. With help from a lemon juice experiment, children learned how hiding the truth is the same as telling a lie. They shared a few true and untrue things about themselves, and then talked about why it's sometimes easier to tell a lie—but how we can't hide the truth from God. God loves it when we tell the truth, and nothing can ever separate us from his love. We damage personal relationships whenever we lie to each other.

Parents: Tell your child about a time you tried to "cover up" something—and what happened. Perhaps it was a mistake you made or something about yourself you didn't want others to know, such as a habit of biting your fingernails. Encourage your child to talk honestly about something he or she may be tempted to cover up. As you listen with understanding rather than shock, you'll encourage your child to walk in the truth in the future as well.

God, thank you for loving us! Help us always be honest with each other. In Jesus' name. Amen.

Celebration Place Journal

Sad   Mad   Glad   Afraid

This week was...

_____

_____

✏ Write About It...

1. _____

_____

2. _____

_____

3. _____

_____

🙏 Pray About It...

_____

_____

_____

WEEK 17: SPONSOR

Key Verse: "Happy are the pure in heart" (Matthew 5:8).

THIS WEEK AT CELEBRATION PLACE

Your child learned that people need each other to be encouragers. That's why our church has Celebrate Recovery, where special people serve as sponsors to help others stand strong every day. Children practiced giving each other compliments, high fives, and other positive reinforcements, and then talked about how it feels to be both the giver and recipient of encouragement.

Parents: Share with your child one thing your sponsor does to encourage you. Perhaps your sponsor calls regularly, has a great sense of humor, or listens without judging. You can be general or specific about your sponsor with your child. Ask your child if there's a special leader or friend at Celebration Place who's particularly encouraging to him or her. Thank your child for being supportive of you, and give specific examples of that encouragement.

 God, thank you for putting people in our lives to encourage and support us. Help us support other people, too. In Jesus' name, Amen.

Celebration Place Journal

Sad   Mad   Glad   Afraid

This week was...

_____
_____

✎ Write About It...

1. _____
_____

2. _____
_____

3. _____
_____

🙏 Pray About It...

_____
_____
_____

WEEK 18: SPONSOR

Key Verse: "Happy are the pure in heart" (Matthew 5:8).

THIS WEEK AT CELEBRATION PLACE

Your child learned that we can help each other do hard things, just like Jesus our ultimate sponsor helps us. We can turn to Jesus for encouragement any time, any place. Children learned that encouragement helps us keep our hearts soft. They learned the importance of thanking others who support them. Kids were challenged to help a friend or family member this week with a simple act such as sharing something or baking a treat.

Parents: Tell about a time you went out of your way to do something kind for someone else. How did the person receive your kindness? Talk about how it feels to be appreciated and to know you've encouraged someone. Then help your child follow through on his or her idea to encourage someone this week.

God, we couldn't do anything without you! Thank you for the best encourager of all: Jesus. In Jesus' name. Amen.

Celebration Place Journal

Sad **Mad** **Glad** **Afraid**

This week was...

_____
_____

✏️ **Write About It...**

1. _____
   _____
2. _____
   _____
3. _____
   _____

🙏 **Pray About It...**

_____
_____
_____

WEEK 19: INVENTORY

Key Verse: "Happy are the pure in heart" (Matthew 5:8).

THIS WEEK AT CELEBRATION PLACE

Your child learned that we can ask God to change our character for the better—he'll help us put on a "new self." Children learned that God gives us a list of positive character qualities in Galatians 5:22-23 and that we each decide our character traits. They took an inventory of their character traits from before they began the Celebration Place journey and one with the changes they've seen so far (or hope to see), and then shared with a partner.

Parents: Tell your child one or two positive character traits you see in him or her. Use the list from Galatians 5:22-23 if you want: love, joy, peace, patience, kindness, goodness, faithfulness, gentleness, and self-control. Then explain to your child one of the qualities where God is helping you make positive changes. Invite your child to share his or her "before and after" list with you, and affirm your child's many positive choices.

God, thank you for changing us. Help us put on a new self. In Jesus' name. Amen.

Celebration Place Journal

Sad   Mad   Glad   Afraid

This week was...

_____

_____

Write About It...

1. _____

_____

2. _____

_____

3. _____

_____

Pray About It...

_____

_____

_____

WEEK 20: INVENTORY

Key Verse: "Happy are the pure in heart" (Matthew 5:8).

THIS WEEK AT CELEBRATION PLACE

Your child learned that we choose our own character traits—including how we deal with anger. God wants us to forgive others the same way he forgives us. Children learned that people who hurt them aren't bad people; they're people who've also been hurt. We all have scars from hurts. To deal with hurt, children learned to ask God to help them choose forgiveness and to turn the other cheek.

Parents: Show your child a scar on your body and tell the story behind it. Encourage your child to show you a scar and tell the story behind it, too. Encourage your child to talk about any hidden scars in his or her heart. Be open to your child's hurt feelings and scars; ask for forgiveness if they were caused by you.

 God, thank you for healing our scars. Help us heal our hurts by forgiving people who've hurt us. In Jesus' name. Amen.

Celebration Place Journal

Sad   Mad   Glad   Afraid

This week was...

_____

_____

✏️ write About It...

1. _____

_____

2. _____

_____

3. _____

_____

🙏 Pray About It...

_____

_____

_____

WEEK 21: SPECIAL EVENT

Key Verse: "When we were utterly helpless, Christ came at just the
right time and died for us sinners. Now, most people would not be
willing to die for an upright person, though some might perhaps
be willing to die for a person who is especially good. But God
showed his great love for us by sending Christ to die for us while
we were still sinners" (Romans 5:6-8).

THIS WEEK AT CELEBRATION PLACE

Your child learned that God never stops seeking friendship with
us, just as Marlin never stopping seeking his son Nemo—no matter
the challenges in his path. Even when we ignore God's rules, God
doesn't give up on us. Children learned that God always seeks a
relationship with us so we can live with him forever in heaven. We
can find our way home through Jesus.

Parents: Tell your child about a time you were lost.

Maybe you were separated from your parents in a big department
store or as an adult you couldn't find your way around a new town.
Talk about how sometimes you may feel lost in life but God helps
you find your way.

 *God, thank you for providing a map for following you and
for being there when we lose our way. Help us remember to
seek you. In Jesus' name. Amen.*

Celebration Place Journal

Sad   **Mad**   **Glad**   **Afraid**

This week was...

_____

_____

✏️ Write About It...

1. _____

_____

2. _____

_____

3. _____

_____

🙏 Pray About It...

_____

_____

_____

WEEK 22: SPIRITUAL INVENTORY

Key Verse: "Happy are the pure in heart" (Matthew 5:8).

THIS WEEK AT CELEBRATION PLACE

Your child learned that God wants us to forgive others and to ask for forgiveness when we've done wrong—that includes asking Jesus for forgiveness when we sin. Yet, it's not enough to ask for forgiveness; we need to change, too. Children learned that we can get tangled up on the inside when we don't forgive others, and that Jesus forgives us even when we don't deserve it. Children practiced asking for forgiveness and saying, "I forgive you."

Parents: Describe a time you were angry with someone and how that felt. For example, perhaps a friend made you so angry the two of you didn't speak for a while. Then talk about a time you forgave someone—perhaps the same person and how that felt. Ask your child if there's someone he or she would like to forgive today—and how to best do that.

God, help us forgive others as you forgive us. In Jesus' name. Amen.

Celebration Place Journal

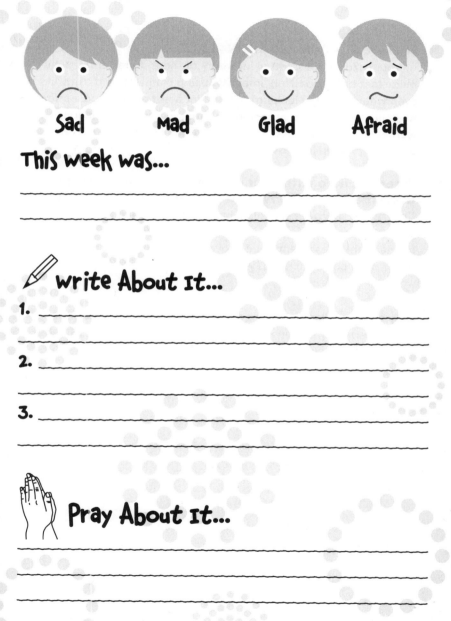

Sad   Mad   Glad   Afraid

This week was...

_____
_____

Write About It...

1. _____
_____
2. _____
_____
3. _____
_____

Pray About It...

_____
_____

WEEK 23: SPIRITUAL INVENTORY

Key Verse: "Happy are the pure in heart" (Matthew 5:8).

THIS WEEK AT CELEBRATION PLACE

Your child took a spiritual inventory of these character traits: humility (not being boastful), integrity (being blameless and truthful, even when no one is looking), and willingness to make God a priority in life (not being so busy that we squeeze out God). Children learned why each of these traits is important to God and talked about ways to build these character qualities.

Parents: Share with your child which of the character traits mentioned above you've grown in the most at Celebrate Recovery. Explain how God has helped you in this area. Then share with your child how you've seen him or her grow in one of the areas mentioned above. Encouraging your child is one of the most powerful things you can do.

 God, we know you love us even though we're not perfect. Thank you for the example of Jesus and for your words in the Bible to help us. In Jesus' name. Amen.

Celebration Place Journal

Sad   Mad   Glad   Afraid

This week was...

_____

_____

✏️ Write About It...

1. _____

_____

2. _____

_____

3. _____

_____

🙏 Pray About It...

_____

_____

_____

WEEK 24: SPIRITUAL INVENTORY

Key Verse: "Happy are the pure in heart" (Matthew 5:8).

THIS WEEK AT CELEBRATION PLACE

Your child thought about God-honoring choices for his or her mind, body, and family. God gave us each of these gifts, and we show our gratitude by taking care of them. Children examined choices we make about guarding our minds by not exposing them to "garbage," protecting our bodies by keeping them clean and pure, and honoring our families by being honest. We need God to help us with this tall order!

Parents: Tell your child what a treasure he or she is to you. Explain why your child is so special to you, and that the Bible says children are a gift from God. Tell your child what a gift he or she is to your family and why you'll always treasure him or her.

God, you give us amazing gifts! Help us appreciate these gifts and take care of them. In Jesus' name. Amen.

Celebration Place Journal

Sad   Mad   Glad   Afraid

This week was...

_____

_____

✏ Write About It...

1. _____

_____

2. _____

_____

3. _____

_____

🙏 Pray About It...

_____

_____

_____

WEEK 25: PRAYER STATIONS

Key Verse: "Happy are the pure in heart" (Matthew 5:8).

THIS WEEK AT CELEBRATION PLACE

Moving through five prayer stations, your child silently talked and listened to God. Children prayed about these topics at the themed stations: relationships that need healing, troubled feelings and thoughts, stress and pressure, forgiving others, and the peace Jesus offers. Children also got an opportunity to commit or recommit their lives to Jesus by placing a nail in a cross.

Parents: Share with your child a prayer that God answered. Ask your child what he or she prayed about at the prayer stations. Then explain what it's like for you to talk to God. Let your child share a recent prayer that God answered or one he or she is still patiently waiting on.

God, your timing is always perfect, and we thank you for knowing just what we need and hearing our prayers. Help us trust you this week. In Jesus' name. Amen.

Celebration Place Journal

Sad **Mad** **Glad** **Afraid**

This week was...

_____
_____

write About It...

1. _____
_____
2. _____
_____
3. _____
_____

Pray About It...

_____
_____
_____

WEEK 28: ADMIT

Key Verse: "Happy are the pure in heart" (Matthew 5:8).

THIS WEEK AT CELEBRATION PLACE

Your child learned that admitting our sins to one another frees us, much like breaking free from chains that weigh us down. Keeping our sins a secret can make our souls feel sick. With courage, we can tell our sins to God so we can be healthy again. Children learned that admitting sins can be hard, but walking around with guilty feelings is much harder.

Parents: Talk about a time you admitted a sin to a friend. For example, maybe you admitted making up an excuse to not hang out or taking something that didn't belong to you. Explain to your child what happened. Talk about how it feels to be able to admit your sins to God and know he'll always forgive you. Encourage your child to feel confident admitting his or her sins to God for forgiveness—and let your child know you'll always listen and support him or her, too.

God, thank you for giving us people we can talk to, and thank you for always listening, too. In Jesus' name. Amen.

Celebration Place Journal

Sad	Mad	Glad	Afraid

This week was...

_____

_____

✏️ Write About It...

1. _____

2. _____

3. _____

🙏 Pray About It...

_____

_____

WEEK 29: READY

Key Verse: "Happy are those whose greatest desire is to do what God requires" (Matthew 5:6).

THIS WEEK AT CELEBRATION PLACE

Your child learned about getting ready to let God work in him or her. Getting ready means being humble and recognizing that we need God to change us. Using the model of a flower, children talked about how healthy roots lead to healthy, beautiful lives. They learned that sins are symptoms behind real issues and worked on figuring out possible root problems that need healing.

Parents: Talk about the biggest change you've made this year. Maybe you've changed jobs or homes. Or perhaps your attitudes and habits have changed as a result of Celebrate Recovery. Talk to your child about how you felt before and after the change. Ask your child to tell the biggest change he or she has made this year. Thank your child for helping you make good choices and supporting you while God works on your inside.

God, help us stay healthy on the inside and the out. Help us be willing to work on problems and be honest with and supportive of each other. Thank you for doing amazing things in our lives. In Jesus' name. Amen.

Celebration Place Journal

Sad   **Mad**   **Glad**   **Afraid**

This week was...

_____

_____

✏️ Write About It...

1. _____

_____

2. _____

_____

3. _____

_____

🙏 Pray About It...

_____

_____

_____

WEEK 30: READY

Key Verse: "Happy are those whose greatest desire is to do what God requires" (Matthew 5:6).

THIS WEEK AT CELEBRATION PLACE

Your child learned that being ready to let God work in our lives takes courage. When we're ready to let God be the leader in our lives, we have to let him take charge. Children also learned that it's important to recognize the real God, who's loving, gracious, and kind—never angry or frightening.

Parents: Talk about a time you knew you were ready for a change. Perhaps you wanted to change schools when you were a child or jobs when you were older. How did you know you were ready for the change? How did you feel during and after the change? How was that like or unlike what it feels like when God is at work in you, making changes? Then invite your child to share changes he or she is experiencing and how that feels.

God, thank you for your love and for sending others to help us on our path. In Jesus' name. Amen.

Celebration Place Journal

Sad   Mad   Glad   Afraid

This week was...

_____
_____

✏ Write About It...

1. _____
_____

2. _____
_____

3. _____
_____

🙏 Pray About It...

_____
_____
_____

WEEK 31: VICTORY

Key Verse: "Happy are those whose greatest desire is to do what God requires" (Matthew 5:6).

THIS WEEK AT CELEBRATION PLACE

Your child learned that we can all make choices to win over our challenges—and none of us has to do it alone. When things get tough, we can depend on Jesus to make us winners. Kids played games to learn about making choices and choosing strategies for victory, and to reinforce that it's easier to win when they have help.

Parents: Describe a time you needed help to win at something. Maybe your team needed someone to score a winning point or you needed help with a project at work. How did you work together to win? Then talk about how it feels to know that God will never let you down, even when the path to victory seems long and challenging. Ask your child about a big win he or she is hoping for. What challenges does he or she have to overcome? Offer to be on the team!

 God, we're so glad you're always on our team! Help us make good choices so we can have victory over challenges in our lives every day. In Jesus' name. Amen.

Celebration Place Journal

Sad **Mad** **Glad** **Afraid**

This week was...

_____

_____

✏️ Write About It...

1. _____

_____

2. _____

_____

3. _____

_____

🙏 Pray About It...

_____

_____

_____

WEEK 33: AMENDS

Key Verse: "Happy are the merciful" and "Happy are the peacemakers" (Matthew 5:7, 9).

THIS WEEK AT CELEBRATION PLACE

Your child learned what it means to make amends—making something right with someone we've hurt. We all sin sometimes, so we all need to ask for forgiveness and make amends when we do. Children learned that God wants them to encourage and forgive others who are trying to make amends. Not forgiving causes bitterness inside, which can make us captives to sin.

Parents: Tell your child about something you broke and tried to fix. If you still have it, such as a dented automobile or a cell phone that went through the wash, show it to your child. Explain how you tried to fix the item and whether you were successful. Then tell your child how it feels to have God's help when it comes to fixing the things in your life.

 God, we need your help in making amends in our relationships...sometimes it's really hard to do by ourselves. Thank you for forgiving us and helping us to forgive others. In Jesus' name. Amen.

Celebration Place Journal

Sad **Mad** **Glad** **Afraid**

This week was...

_____

_____

✏️ Write About It...

1. _____

_____

2. _____

_____

3. _____

_____

🙏 Pray About It...

_____

_____

_____

WEEK 34: SPECIAL EVENT

Key Verse: "This is my commandment: Love each other in the same way I have loved you. There is no greater love than to lay down one's life for one's friends" (John 15:12-13).

THIS WEEK AT CELEBRATION PLACE

Your child learned about the gift of friendship while viewing and discussing the movie *Homeward Bound: The Incredible Journey,* about three family pets devoted to each other. Children learned that real friends laugh together, encourage one another, are loyal when times get tough, and do what's best for each other. Jesus is our best friend—he gave his life for us—and we can respond to his gift of friendship by being his friend in return.

Parents: Tell about your best childhood friend. Share a few memories about how you laughed together, encouraged each other, and put each other first. Then talk with your child about how it feels to know that Jesus gave his life for you and will never, ever let you down, even when times are hard. Ask your child about his or her best friend and the things they do for each other. What would a movie about their friendship look like?

 God, thank you for the friends you put in our lives and for our most special and loving friend, Jesus. Help us be a good friend to Jesus, too. In Jesus' name. Amen.

Celebration Place Journal

Sad   Mad   Glad   Afraid

This week was...

_____

_____

✏️ Write About It...

1. _____

_____

2. _____

_____

3. _____

_____

🙏 Pray About It...

_____

_____

_____

WEEK 35: FORGIVENESS

Key Verse: "Happy are the merciful" and "Happy are the peacemakers" (Matthew 5:7, 9).

THIS WEEK AT CELEBRATION PLACE

Your child learned that we forgive others because it feels good in our hearts...and because it's what God wants us to do. The longer we wait to forgive, the harder it is to do. Children made colorful candy necklaces as reminders of God's gift of forgiveness: purple for Jesus' bruises caused by our sin, red licorice for the blood he shed, white for the clean slate of forgiveness, green for growing in faith, and yellow for heaven's streets of gold.

Parents: Describe the thing that's hardest for you to wait for. Perhaps it's waiting in the grocery line, waiting for Christmas, or waiting for someone to get ready. Then explain how it feels to know you never have to wait for God's forgiveness. Invite your child to talk about whether he or she is waiting to forgive or be forgiven, how it feels, and whether you can help.

God, thank you for sending Jesus so we could be forgiven. Help us not wait to forgive others. In Jesus' name. Amen.

Celebration Place Journal

Sad　Mad　Glad　Afraid

This week was...

_____
_____

✏️ Write About It...

1. _____
_____

2. _____
_____

3. _____
_____

🙏 Pray About It...

_____
_____
_____

WEEK 36: FORGIVENESS

Key Verse: "Happy are the merciful" and "Happy are the peacemakers" (Matthew 5:7, 9).

THIS WEEK AT CELEBRATION PLACE

Your child learned about Jesus' death and resurrection by participating in a re-enactment of Luke 22–24—the story of Jesus' death and resurrection. Through retelling these Scriptures, children heard about the extent of Jesus' love and mercy; if he could forgive those who betrayed him during his trial and crucifixion, then his forgiveness is truly beyond measure. Children learned that we can ask Jesus to forgive all our sins.

Parents: Talk with your child about the most amazing things you can both imagine. How deep is the deepest ocean? How loud is the loudest noise? How beautiful is the most beautiful sight? How tall is the tallest mountain? Then share how it feels to know that Jesus' love and forgiveness for you is greater—more immeasurable—than all of those things combined! Ask your child what problem he or she thinks might be too big for God to handle, if any. Then reassure your child of God's infinite love and power.

 God, whether our problems feel big or small, we know that your love for us is huge and endless—and you'll forgive us if we just ask. In Jesus' name. Amen.

Celebration Place Journal

Sad   **Mad**   **Glad**   **Afraid**

This week was...

_____

_____

✏️ Write About It...

1. _____

_____

2. _____

_____

3. _____

_____

🙏 Pray About It...

_____

_____

_____

WEEK 37: GRACE

Key Verse: "Happy are the merciful" and "Happy are the peacemakers" (Matthew 5:7, 9).

THIS WEEK AT CELEBRATION PLACE

Your child learned about the concept of grace—and that God wants us to share his grace with others. Grace is reaching out to someone and loving that person even with all his or her imperfections, so that person might experience joy and love more fully. Grace is showing God's kindness. Children got to show grace to others, especially new kids at Celebration Place.

Parents: Tell about a time you were the "new kid." Perhaps you were in a new school or just joined a church. How did it feel to wonder whether others would accept you as you were? Who reached out to you in grace? Then share with your child how it feels to know that God accepts you—just as you are, flaws and all. Invite your child to talk about how kids have shown him or her grace and how to show it to others.

God, you've shown us so much grace. Please help us to show your grace to others this week. In Jesus' name. Amen.

Celebration Place Journal

Sad   **Mad**   **Glad**   **Afraid**

This week was...

_____

_____

✏️ Write About It...

1. _____

_____

2. _____

_____

3. _____

_____

🙏 Pray About It...

_____

_____

_____

WEEK 38: GRACE

Key Verse: "Happy are the merciful" and "Happy are the peacemakers" (Matthew 5:7, 9).

THIS WEEK AT CELEBRATION PLACE

By hearing how Jesus touched and healed a leper, your child learned about what it means to be merciful. Children talked about their ability to have mercy on others, including their families, as their families journey through recovery. We all need grace and mercy—from others and from God—to help us come out of the darkness and into his light.

Parents: Tell about a time you felt like a leper. Perhaps there was a time you felt left out as a child, or as an adult your family didn't include you in a gathering. Tell your child what that experience was like for you. Talk with your child about when he or she may feel like a leper. Encourage your child that God loves both of you always and welcomes you into his family.

God, thank you for always loving us and showing us how to love others. In Jesus' name. Amen.

Celebration Place Journal

Sad   Mad   Glad   Afraid

This week was...

_____

_____

✏️ Write About It...

1. _____

_____

2. _____

_____

3. _____

_____

🙏 Pray About It...

_____

_____

_____

WEEK 39: PRAYER STATIONS

Key Verse: "Happy are the merciful" and "Happy are the peacemakers" (Matthew 5:7, 9).

THIS WEEK AT CELEBRATION PLACE

Your child learned that God's light can shine through the broken places in our lives, like sunlight through a cracked vase, making our hearts grow strong and creating beauty in our lives. Then children experienced Jesus at prayer stations, silently asking God to come into the broken areas of their lives—where they've been hurt and where they need forgiveness. Together they prayed and thanked God for his grace and mercy.

Parents: Show or tell about something you made better by fixing. Maybe you picked up an old bike at a yard sale and made it the coolest on the block with some paint and a few well-placed stickers. Then share how you've experienced God's light shining through broken areas in your life. Tell your child the light that you see streaming through his or her life.

 God, thank you for the beauty you create in the broken areas of our lives where we have hurts or sins. Help us be your light to others. In Jesus' name. Amen.

Celebration Place Journal

Sad   Mad   Glad   Afraid

This week was...

_____

_____

✏️ Write About It...

1. _____

_____

2. _____

_____

3. _____

_____

🙏 Pray About It...

_____

_____

_____

WEEK 40: CROSSROADS

Key Verse: "So, if you think you are standing firm, be careful that you don't fall!" (1 Corinthians 10:12).

THIS WEEK AT CELEBRATION PLACE

Your child reflected on the Celebration Place journey so far and took time to rest and quietly listen to God. Children considered any crossroads they're at, and they found encouragement to keep moving forward. The decision to move forward and not turn back rests with each of us. Children also played a game to practice "standing firm" and talked about how they can face the challenge to stand firm in life.

Parents: Talk about a time you were at a crossroads.

This could be any important decision you had to make: which career path to take or whether to move across the country, for example. Describe whether it was difficult or easy to stand firm in your decision. Then talk about how it feels to make a conscious decision to let God guide you at the crossroads in life. Ask your child what he or she thinks might be the hardest part about standing firm during the journey ahead, and pledge your support.

God, please guide us now as we do our best to stand firm in life. In Jesus' name. Amen.

Celebration Place Journal

Sad　　**Mad**　　**Glad**　　**Afraid**

This week was...

Sad because, I thought about my dad.

✏️ Write About It...

1. I think it was was hard and I couldn't do it.
2. I think its imposible to fly.
3. I have what it take if I keep trying.

🙏 Pray About It...

I would pray about not having my mom and dad to not have a divores

WEEK 41: CROSSROADS

Key Verse: "So, if you think you are standing firm, be careful that you don't fall!" (1 Corinthians 10:12).

THIS WEEK AT CELEBRATION PLACE

Your child learned that he or she has a decision to make when arriving at a crossroads, which happens every day. We can change our lives by the choices we make. Children learned that while God made each of us different, he gave us the ability to choose the right way and to treat others the right way; growing in knowledge and understanding of God will help us discern what's best.

Parents: Describe a choice you have a hard time making. Maybe you can't decide what to make for dinner or what book to check out at the library. Talk about how choosing one thing means leaving other choices behind. Then talk about the choice you make to follow God every day and what things you have to let go of when you make that decision. Ask your child to tell you about one way he or she has chosen to follow God in the past week.

 God, thank you for helping us learn how to follow you. Help us depend on you to make good choices. In Jesus' name. Amen.

Celebration Place Journal

Sad **Mad** **Glad** **Afraid**

This week was...

_____

_____

Write About It...

1. _____

_____

2. _____

_____

3. _____

_____

Pray About It...

_____

_____

_____

WEEK 42: SPECIAL EVENT

Key Verse: "In his grace, God has given us different gifts for doing certain things well. So if God has given you the ability to prophesy, speak out with as much faith as God has given you. If your gift is serving others, serve them well. If you are a teacher, teach well. If your gift is to encourage others, be encouraging. If it is giving, give generously. If God has given you leadership ability, take the responsibility seriously. And if you have a gift for showing kindness to others, do it gladly" (Romans 12:6-8).

THIS WEEK AT CELEBRATION PLACE

Your child watched the movie *Mulan,* about a young Chinese girl who joins the Chinese army and finds that her gifts and skills help make her a hero. Children discussed how God gives us all unique gifts to use for serving others, and children learned they can encourage others to use their gifts. They saw that when Mulan used her gifts, everyone benefited.

Parents: Tell your child about a good gift you've received. Ask your child to tell about a good gift also. Then talk about a gift God has given you to serve others and honor him. Ask your child what gifts he or she has; build up and encourage your child with your own observations about his or her gifts.

God, you've blessed us with amazing gifts and we thank you for that. Help us use these gifts to honor you and serve other people. In Jesus' name. Amen.

Celebration Place Journal

Sad   Mad   Glad   Afraid

This week was...

_____

_____

Write About It...

1. _____

_____

2. _____

_____

3. _____

_____

Pray About It...

_____

_____

WEEK 43: DAILY INVENTORY

Key Verse: "So, if you think you are standing firm, be careful that you don't fall!" (1 Corinthians 10:12).

THIS WEEK AT CELEBRATION PLACE

Your child learned how important it is to check in with God every day about how he or she is doing. This constant connection with God helps us make positive choices daily, which helps us make good choices rather than just react to people and events. Children also learned that choosing God daily means to love him with all our heart, soul, and mind—and to love others as ourselves.

Parents: Talk to your child about how you take an inventory of your life. Tell your child about how you measure the positive qualities you're working on in your life daily. Ask your child how checking in with God helps him or her, and point out some of the positive qualities you see in your child.

God, thank you for being here for us. Help us remember to check in—and say yes to you daily. In Jesus' name. Amen.

Celebration Place Journal

Sad   Mad   Glad   Afraid

This week was...

_____
_____

Write About It...

1. _____
_____
2. _____
_____
3. _____
_____

Pray About It...

_____
_____

WEEK 44: RELAPSE

Key Verse: "Let the Word of Christ dwell in you richly"
(Colossians 3:16).

THIS WEEK AT CELEBRATION PLACE

Your child discovered it's difficult to escape temptation, but God helps us stand strong. Children learned that Jesus gave us the perfect example of how to resist temptation when he used the Word of God against the devil (Matthew 4). When we know God's Word, we're better able to respond and stand strong against temptation. Children practiced running away from negative influences.

Parents: Tell your child about something small that tempts you. For example, maybe you're tempted to sleep in on workdays, or maybe you can't resist chocolate when you're on a diet. Explain why it's so hard to resist that temptation—and what would happen if you didn't stand strong. Then explain how it helps you to know that God will help you stand strong against any temptation if you go to him. Let your child know you're always available to talk about his or her temptations, no matter how large or small.

 God, thank you for sending Jesus to provide the perfect example of how to resist temptation. Help us remember to look to you for help in standing strong. In Jesus' name. Amen.

Celebration Place Journal

Sad   Mad   Glad   Afraid

This week was...

_____

_____

✏️ Write About It...

1. _____

_____

2. _____

_____

3. _____

_____

🙏 Pray About It...

_____

_____

_____

WEEK 45: RELAPSE

**Key Verse: "Let the Word of Christ dwell in you richly"
(Colossians 3:16).**

THIS WEEK AT CELEBRATION PLACE

Your child learned that we all experience moments of temptation that we may not be able to resist. Children created prayer reminders to invite God into their lives when they need a "do-over."
They talked about encouraging each other during relapses and
learned that prayer is more powerful than worrying about difficul-
ties. Together they created a list of things they could pray about.

Parents: Tell about a time you needed a do-over. Perhaps
you had a bad day at school or work, or you hit a bump in the road
in an important relationship. Explain what happened and how you
overcame the relapse. Then talk with your child about how it feels
to stop worrying and instead come to Celebrate Recovery and ask
God for a major do-over with your hurts, hang-ups, and habits.
Remind your child that we all fall down sometimes, and ask what
he or she would like a chance to do over today.

 *God, thank you for being there when we need a do-over
in life. Your love is powerful and amazing! In Jesus' name.
Amen.*

Celebration Place Journal

Sad   Mad   Glad   Afraid

This week was...

_____

_____

✏️ Write About It...

1. _____

_____

2. _____

_____

3. _____

_____

🙏 Pray About It...

_____

_____

_____

WEEK 46: GRATITUDE

Key Verse: "Let the Word of Christ dwell in you richly"
(Colossians 3:16).

THIS WEEK AT CELEBRATION PLACE

Your child read the Bible to see how spending time in God's
Word will help him or her see things differently. Children learned
about gratitude and practiced giving thanks for different areas of
their lives. Through a skit they saw what it looks like when a person
is ungrateful and misses the beauty in everyday blessings.

Parents: Talk about something you're grateful for. For
example, maybe you saw someone who has less than you and it
made you appreciate the things we often take for granted. How
did learning more about others help you appreciate things more?
Then talk about how learning more about God is helping you appreciate and give thanks for all that God has done and continues
to do for you. Talk with your child about his or her commitment to
read the Bible this week, and offer support for following through—
which might include reading together.

*God, the more we learn about you, the more we grow to un-
derstand how much you've done for us. Thank you for your
many gifts to us. In Jesus' name. Amen.*

Celebration Place Journal

Sad   Mad   Glad   Afraid

This week was...

_____

_____

✏️ Write About It...

1. _____

_____

2. _____

_____

3. _____

_____

🙏 Pray About It...

_____

_____

_____

WEEK 47: GRATITUDE

**Key Verse: "Let the Word of Christ dwell in you richly"
(Colossians 3:16).**

THIS WEEK AT CELEBRATION PLACE

Your child learned that it's important to show God gratitude for all he's done for us. Children discussed things they're thankful for that they can experience through their five senses (in other words, things money can't buy), and they talked about how to give thanks for those things. They made "Gratitude Lists" and considered how to keep life's busyness from crowding out their thankfulness.

Parents: Talk about a gift from God that's easy to take for granted. Maybe it's easy to forget to thank God for food on your table, for example. What reminds you to be grateful, and how can you show your appreciation? Then talk about how Celebrate Recovery is helping you appreciate Jesus for the power he has to change your life—and all you have to do is invite him in. Invite your child to share things he or she thanks God for, and encourage or help your child to finish the Gratitude List from Celebration Place this week. Then post the list in your home.

 God, today we thank you for...(Take turns listing things with your child.) And mostly, thank you for your power to change our lives. In Jesus' name. Amen.

Celebration Place Journal

Sad   **Mad**   **Glad**   **Afraid**

This week was...

_____

_____

✏️ Write About It...

1. _____

_____

2. _____

_____

3. _____

_____

🙏 Pray About It...

_____

_____

_____

WEEK 48: GIVE

Key Verse: "Happy are those who are persecuted because they do what God requires" (Matthew 5:10).

THIS WEEK AT CELEBRATION PLACE

Your child learned from Jesus' example of washing his disciples' feet what it means to really give to others. Children played a game to practice sharing with others in need and talked about how it feels to give and to receive. Kids discovered how God wants us to give his love to others, and they took on the challenge to share the good news about God with someone this week.

Parents: Tell your favorite way to give to others. Maybe you love to bake for others, or maybe you're always willing to baby-sit for a friend. Describe how it feels to serve others. Then talk about how it feels to hear the good news about Jesus in Celebrate Recovery and to share the gift of that news with others. Ask your child if he or she would like to tell a friend about God's love this week, and offer to pray for that friend. Encourage your child to tell about God's love using his or her favorite way of giving—for example, if your child likes to draw, help create a card for someone and include a message about God.

God, thank you for giving us lots of love to spread around. Help us share the good news about you to someone who needs to hear about you this week. In Jesus' name. Amen.

Celebration Place Journal

Sad **Mad** **Glad** **Afraid**

This week was...

_____

_____

Write About It...

1. _____

_____

2. _____

_____

3. _____

_____

Pray About It...

_____

_____

WEEK 49: GIVE

Key Verse: "Happy are those who are persecuted because they do what God requires" (Matthew 5:10).

THIS WEEK AT CELEBRATION PLACE

Your child learned from Jesus' example of being kind to the dishonest tax collector that mercy is the greatest gift we can give others. Jesus said, "Healthy people don't need a doctor—sick people do." People who hurt us need to feel God's forgiveness. Children learned that they can let their light shine like Jesus by being merciful and kind to others.

Parents: Tell about a time you were kind this week. For example, maybe someone at the grocery store seemed agitated and hurried, and you let that person go ahead of you in line. Describe how it felt to show that kindness. Then talk about how it feels to know that the greatest gift God gives you is forgiveness, and that you can share it with others by shining his light of forgiveness.

God, help us shine your light by being merciful to others this week. In Jesus' name. Amen.

Celebration Place Journal

Sad   Mad   Glad   Afraid

This week was...

_____

_____

✏️ Write About It...

1. _____

_____

2. _____

_____

3. _____

_____

🙏 Pray About It...

_____

_____

_____

WEEK 50: YES

Key Verse: "Happy are those who are persecuted because they do what God requires" (Matthew 5:10).

THIS WEEK AT CELEBRATION PLACE

Your child learned that we each have a choice to say yes or no to God. Saying yes fills our hearts with good things; saying no causes hurts. Children used creative ways to imagine and create stories of ways they could say yes to God: a movie outline, an artist's rendering, and a story with props. They had an opportunity to share their stories with one another.

Parents: Tell about a time you said yes to God and something amazing happened. You might choose to tell how saying yes to the Celebrate Recovery journey has changed your life. Then share with your child how it feels to know that God gives you the choice to say yes to him every day. Invite your child to tell a story about how his or her life has been changed by saying yes to God.

 God, thank you for helping us patch the hurts in our lives. Help us continue to say yes to you every day. In Jesus' name. Amen.

Celebration Place Journal

Sad   **Mad**   **Glad**   **Afraid**

This week was...

_____

_____

write About It...

1. _____

_____

2. _____

_____

3. _____

_____

Pray About It...

_____

_____

_____

WEEK 51: YES

Key Verse: "Happy are those who are persecuted because they do what God requires" (Matthew 5:10).

THIS WEEK AT CELEBRATION PLACE

Your child learned that all of God's gifts are good, even if some of them might not seem so good at first. We've all had gifts like that—for instance, a bulky scarf that didn't seem so great at a summer birthday, but that really came in handy when cold weather came. Kids learned how important it is to be open to receiving God's gifts. They got to open gifts—one in a sloppy package and one in a beautiful package to compare what was inside. They got to play with oozy goo—and compare that to how solid a rock God is. Then they were challenged to do the impossible—and think about how powerful our God is.

Parents: Tell about a time one of God's gifts didn't seem good at first. Maybe you lost a job and you felt terrible, but then you got a job you liked even better or you got to spend time learning something new. Describe how you came to realize the gift was good. Then share about how coming to Celebrate Recovery has brought positive changes to your life—changes that help you say yes to God one day at a time. Ask your child what has surprised him or her most about coming to Celebration Station and saying yes to God.

 God, thank you for the best gift of all—your Son, Jesus. Help us remember to say yes to you every day as we remember the many great gifts you give us. In Jesus' name. Amen.

Celebration Place Journal

Sad **Mad** **Glad** **Afraid**

This week was...

_____
_____

✏️ Write About It...

1. _____
_____

2. _____
_____

3. _____
_____

🙏 Pray About It...

_____
_____
_____

WEEK 52: CELEBRATION

THIS WEEK AT CELEBRATION PLACE

Children celebrated all that God has done for them at Celebration Place. Our theme was "learning to fill the empty spots in our lives with Jesus"—in a room filled with spots and dots of all shapes and sizes, including snacks and games. We talked about how there's no substitute for God, no matter how hard we try to fill those empty spots with other things. Children learned they can choose God to connect the dots in their lives.

Parents: Talk about the connection you've made at Celebrate Recovery. Discuss how you can see the path of "dots" when you look back. Perhaps someone invited you or you found a flier at church. Then talk about how it feels to know that choosing God and Celebrate Recovery could help you fill the empty spots in your life. Ask your child how he or she would like to celebrate how God has helped your family on your journey to recovery. Then celebrate together! Anyone up for ice cream?

 God, please help us remember to invite you into our hearts and share your light with others—we need you every day of our lives. In Jesus' name. Amen.